Sound Rituals

Jim Leftwich and billy bob beamer

mOnocle-Lash Anti-Press
February 2018
Roanoke , Virginia

Some of these Sound Rituals appeared in the following online publications:

textimagepoem, edited by jim leftwich
slowforward, edited by marco giovenale
experiential-experimental, edited by Volodymyr Bilyk

cover image by Jim Leftwich & Bill Beamer

mOnocle anti-press

Jan. A.Da. 102 A.H. 188
2018 A.D.

mOnocle-Lash Anti-Press
monoclelash.wordpress.com
monoclelash@gmail.com

FORWARD

Jim Leftwich and billy bob beamer call these complex and playful poems Sound Rituals. In a letter, Leftwich says, "I got the title from an article about a Cecil Taylor performance from the 1980s. In some of his live recordings, he seems to build the structure for his improvisations during the performance itself. Certain kinds of poems can be written that way as well....In a sense, the writing of a poem is always a sound ritual, and the collaborative writing of a poem is even more so." These poems function, then, not only as sound poems, but as everything that can happen in poetry: they are visual, surreal, lyrical, political, thoughtful, expressionistic, intimate, literary, collaborative, improvisational, and much else. The sound or sonoric dimension, nevertheless, is quite strong, and is present in the rhyming, in the echoing of vowels and consonants, and in the practice of transduction or homophonic translation. The "ritual" aspect of these works perhaps refers to the way they were created, as a specific process between two people – a collaboration – but it also suggests a way to read or perform them: as a kind of multivalent incantation, an ambiguous text that provides new meanings and resonances every time it is accessed.

"Sound Ritual Number 55" exemplifies many of these characteristics. It opens with the phrase "masks of sound/and tarotic unrest" which seems to refer to speech as a mask emitting signs to be interpreted, "under a curvilinear seaside". That is, as a proteic interpretation, ever-changing. That idea is reinforced by the reference, a few lines down, to the astrologer and alchemist Paracelsus, one of several specific cultural references, such as "Popeye", "Hercules", and "Bird" (Charlie Parker comes to mind). The poem also plays with words, for example in the neologisms "herculuckier" and "buzzcouping", and plays with sounds: "scoups/snoops/couping", "buzz/fuzz", "Paraclete/Paracelsus", and "sound/unbound/unwound".

Flies become birds in an alchemical frenzy! There is, in addition, a sense of place in this poem, a sense of sea and wide spaces, and of voices that open and expand into that space. It is fascinating that those voices seem light and positive, even while being "praise-songs of the heretics/burning at their stakes". This is one of the most striking things about this book, that in spite of the historical and contemporary horrors of which it is strongly aware, it is so confident and life-affirming. Leftwich says that this apparently paradoxical aspect of this book, and its "improvisational, processual, often letteral poetry can provide a situation, and a process" which could function "for both writers and readers" presumably as a way of finding a kind of understanding of the world and the mind that creates and/or perceives it.

These unique and wonderfully flexible poems can, and should, be read and contemplated by a reader in his or her solitude, but they would also, it seems to me, make marvelous performance texts, which could be performed by two or more persons. In fact, some kind of choral performance, with many voices, would concord with the very nature of these works, which seem to have been created by a plurality of voices, voices very much in consort with each other.

John M. Bennett
January 2018

sound ritual number one

...too easily brought to mean
anything,   either for you or
for me,   even if it ever was
  Or never was 2 tip the day
To be a vertical motion to be
Where.   I.   Sitin
The "blue hair of the mountain"
ears swirl to meat the forklift.
We wash our lips in the ocean,
where the blue grease ether
events. tethered to wind whip
pingthru the mountain forks
laid out futures meat the soak
ing shilled and shaking bone

november 2017

sound ritual number two

One, to hold nothingmeat
Hostage, nor uneven us,
ourSombr thoughts & vel
Cro underground E- ther.
Two, to fold forevermeat
in half twice, crisp the cri
nkle between thumb and
forefinger, like a thinking
veil. tHree,sheered & *inten*
  se th   *rill thtrick l*ethru th
  toes of the jamof pearlsoff
  orefinger, ...feet and dust,
Fo(u)r meat and shroud-dust,
(F)ive bone-post sour as crow.

november 2017

sound ritual number three

wisp shrinking thumb trickles
  underdown to the vertical
tip pong pointed dawn, sl
it *pardon* downpong *pointe*
d taped mask'd submar in e mus
tachioed green mussed ivy trombone
 bedfordsplash in keyeth dawn, D
            ark
           ness
              ts
                splish
a downpour of starlings amongst
our apple trees, all feathers windows
& dawn a *d*apple breath...
a dapple breath, the pointed pongtip,
      slide if greased...

november 2017

sound ritual number four

mysteries reside in the last half
of the holograph bait bat beet
bet bite bit boat bot butte but
spirit resides in flesh like vowels
in consonants bee buh cee dee
duh eff gee aitch jay kay el em

[under th shaded el~em entry elm]

n~o **P** Q'R[noniss]s aints t opple u nder-
ground *vertical* ?words
        [before thF'all]

X
yr.Z one **z**one
mysteries corral in the second half
baited flesh to consciousness bent

november 2017

sound ritual number five

fog jetty disk tribunal during
        lake vitamin perforated
   coastal azure poetics
rug jelly snark binaural often
        jette redaction hyperion
ether cos mos blindsounding
   birdsong roasted bugs
        jettisoned darkly pure
risks mince slick perfections
onfive goofing meme.
      loblolly/opines. monk
 spins light staccato sandwiches

november 2017

sound ritual number six

technicians of interior out
casts hammerwiggle openmindlanguage
martian expulsion
  HYperion at doh
 doors dot perceptic...
at the *window,* looking in through his Reflection.

Histo from holyrollover   *boeuf/;k* jerky
Hun gonto Fe/ormium mon lit
 dada ona gig onagag ajag gedbredden,
                    looking in through his Intercon
                    nec []tion| Shun
at the *marrow,* tomorrow is only another
                         victory over the sun.

november 2017

sound ritual number seven

mirrorsuspended Texas bringing
coastlines resemble rivers re
semble blood vessels resemble
neurons resemble tree branches
twisting in the muddy pastry claw of it
resembling in mountains reflections of Texas
reassembling brooding vassals re tracing
neu tron stars,   powdermilk
up thru tree branches,
gross wink grinding disguises patched pitched
designs hbidden in plane vewe
hpiqqen hqippen enplained vu

november 2017

sound ritual number eight

stars twitch, rattle from
the futile anemic sky.
switch off the scratch'd
moon in the pooled liver,
sour favor of the botched

tars witch, battle from
inutile asemic thigh.
hitch off the ratchet
spoon mulled river,
flour savor of the notch

arse itch, twaddle not
the ant hill, pansemia nigh
rich off racket from scratch,
tune in the lone survivor,
our saviour's flavor of the catch

sparse niche
wading knots
thanatos pill
pansemic high school
rich golf
pocket form scats
tone in the lune
surf visor
our wavicle's labor
in the batch

november 2017

sound ritual number nine

star stir stair stain
tain tin tine wine
fine fire fare far
tar star
tar star mar car
cane cain laid paid
cur blur fur pure
cure lure liar plier
Sam Patch never
jumped from the
Wasena bridge
into the Roanoke
River

november 2017

sound ritual number ten
ten reduces to one-

burnt orange fall &   ten lady
bugs coagulate like so much blood
fat in the high corners of the workroom
mostly red   they soon
fall,   they drip blood
ten reduced to one
multicavity klystron   a typical
hot-cathode thyratron   resonant
cavity magnetron   Puerto Rico
abandoned without power   rain is
a postcard from god   the hurricane
unearthed ancestral artifacts of the
extinct Calusa tribe shell indians
shellslady bugs   shells as home:
Puerto Rico
if we could be
reduced to one
we would get it
sitting at my desk
staring through
my reflection
at the backyard
beside the alley
it is 8:13 p.m.
and one poem leads to another

november 2017

sound ritual number eleven

osage orange at the keyboard salts
the sign before the church. following,
overwhelming, plucking, building,
yelping, offering, resulting, running,
cavorting, thundering, emitting
blood orange the omnipresent
blunderingskies' dedread heartbeat
 putz
    11:11   11:11
more law of fives || beehive. claw. ore.
i & i. i & i. puttering. beating. heartening.
read unread dread. eyes plundering
blunt underpresents omnivorous. the
killing, selling, shilling, shelling, stalling,
balling, crawling, beating, beating no
heart.putz
    11:11   11:11

november 2017

Sound Ritual #12

poppay rivets cozy carbladz
catunk!, fans, a stenciled cough {]] co
signed in theVultureSand, coterminous withslip
sneezeCel Ray mann. Bluuurrr, as inth de
fence tackles my '62 t rip to the
5 spot with Bernie. Reduction to 4   get it? this gets bother
Tosome....*ocoley* ferron, Batshit! coenties Slip, exhorted o
at dOh los,   eus,   o.dd.   serp,

o say can you see
        by the dawn's early light
1) miniature putz putz golf 2) Adolf's beer hall putz
3) the Putz and Judy Show 4) a 3-hole paper putz
what a funny funky word

like t urd, urn, d urt , dep lete d ust
pu h   tz
        bird bird bird, bird is the word

november 2017

sound ritual number thirteen

alien roar brine breaking floats
tile mud throat collided sea
tentacles the jaws foam
battering their least coast feet
needed the lean browser clocks
t'mile turn boated manacles routes
seen over king lotus' muted crease
tattered before rumor's toasted points
floats sea foam feet clocks routes
crease points tattered spleen smile
bleeding spattered pentangles' file
the 'fame swat' t'cease tentangles
alter board shrine shrieks of goats
a mile in tug-boated Colosseum bleed
ventricles, the pause & glow, battr'dram
lotus boat the lean least jaws collide

november 2017

sound ritual number fourteen

2 tip the day never was
To be a vertical/   motion to be
Where. There. insults''blue hair ears swirl
okkears s.w.i.k oroll eo liftlips
a hitchus out ' dark chambres of nar
cotic eg osimmering, flaggedX, shilled mountain,
Historic photo of the sea bestowed ix 19 N the public
conversat she Char first eye as well as seat them out.
the question reminded. call to mindt horses, botany,
a washing machine, the grassy knoll, the illuminating
gas, 4-ferr household plankton, a secret location
on the lower east side, the man sliding the wall down
seating them, spitting out special numbers with salt, for
bidding, electrical apparitions There   in the jankymoss alley
riders of the purple sage.. midnite riders [get me now
seat them out. with questions rebels now. the skies
blurn vertical purple picture of horses, weeds, a 19C
washer and dryer in pixils. ali seke othern se2?
eating. budding. sliders. beat. blurt. ashes.
eclectic hem of the vortical gemstone.
pixies burp gurgling algae.
decibel snow.
all seek the
southern
sea.

november 2017

Sound Ritual #15

gargle the perfect sea
whirr the robot saddles
faint as flat as a sand cake
in th sub sun cash in fall
c hokey hi on debris yets
ave it split from drowning
barbed stir tainted inch
coded avenue the flat
sub/alt/tern lo fi hi hat
spitting image spun in
pur(e)fect rattlers shut
ters spinning up yr bet
betterwane sandsea up
clouds spin flamboyant
creepygray thumb hitch
switches crumbs sleeping
the day away in buoyant
flames nips clout in the
bud sandcastles made
of butter pinned beneath
the waning moon hut hat
club coded barbarian shave

november 2017

sound ritual number sixteen

asparagus sea sharpner
drum in   A flat   major
policy hard wind tongue
baroque Kiln. by lamp sea
by trumpet litribs aflame
club float bar ring waftalc
valveoilsoakT beeswax at
spit keysome overcome
by religionweptswept out
by diameter accepted the
war ends in its novel not
in the faces on the bus at
the book 0-8 experiends
in the speech-attic minute
prose radio incessantly
asks, hammering on stilts
an asparagus drum.

november 2017

sound ritual #17

taps by the grass, the mar
ble dhead silver brass up
ended dimlydraind shot,he
grinmaged '' “E a sharp al
ways keep a-   b mind... '' Rap
Rapturedetour edod gin geroot
lawn elegy. they mid-since
fifteen embark behind the heart.
traps blended grime. trap
sways blended suture grime.
rummage in marks fork
nails the mindharp. gutwinds
the wrench hammer pliers tow
arc slender blended grime be
hind midsentence embark then
blended detour 15, 'gaps in the
'grass alas'so ,what tuning fork
since midfifteen   elegyTrapshot
ball peen hammer grammar

november 2017

sound ritual number eighteen

who had
dividual
mirrors
cast masks
nakes ubs
rorrim
'no it cel fer'
jections
urim
by thumbs
piano crew
wrecks line
lime subs
titu tethum
um sacks
snacks gum
teeth in
situ
subcultural
timeless
wine

november 2017

sound ritual number nineteen

population thalamus BC clearance imprisoned
linear stems wax/wane knit territorial
harbors drainage conspicuous malkuth leaf
Transitional base hypo alley muss mapped
Smets sheets of paper marked tree rain age
Tugs in maloprompt goof water rolled up.
holds hedge Hurricane north floor tinted
playground saturday Temporarily archaic
to rebuild the nouns with hopes from debt.

november 2017

sound ritual number twenty

waffle kiln
parakeet
spore
ribs
ribbonic
diago/nal
unpunctuated
spiritus
catkin
miter box
Rivera
Carved
Hardsc Dr Dr
spider hole
kinship
spirulina
percolates

november 2017

sound ritual # 21

stuffing wallpaper
fading
roulette singularity
pushing   button
button to buttonup
ending fire road
doogoders coloring bookies
a can con vaca
ncy/\wisp ''blue
hairsea   grout
raiding stiff route cushions
mutton bending dog
codes ashcan
fancy wail
pauper single
lariat butte
futon fire
toad coil luring
coin wasp
hairless sea cookies
vacant blue doubt

november 2017

sound ritual number twenty two

pheromone helium
fig three jalopy om
thunder flashlights
margarita congas
run around in four
a black metalstand
a6pack of blue flats
monitor feedback
pole speakers anon
noon peaks of otter
role feedlot seeded
flits blue Packard
meat in sand "in for
a round run of it"
marginal congress
lights fish under
ombudsman jalopy
for free wig helix
moaning fears

november 2017

sound ritual #23

neck warming the catagory
repealing watermelon roof
tile
a scent
the tall opines and 'odors
bleed
bad moon in the stall & go
& 'there's a bathroom on
the right'
wreck rappelling vile
smile file ascii
creed bed seed & swarming
nighthawks lemon
later cents
the bald mood bat tub
catastrophic Tagore spoof
the tall map less outdoors
at the blackwater revival

november 2017

sound ritual number 24

rabid   slide
jungle chew
thun derst or m
baggage in the floss
lost in the rat glow clan
crawl blather jaw
chaw. chew the raw
law. claw and lather
the crawling can.
low at the ghost in
loss. in the gauge
bag murders dirt.
under hewn bungle
ride the habit.

november 2017

sound ritual #25

soggy rise
motley clippers
zeitgeist donka nip
puritan glaze sleazers
sneakers in cabinets
spongers --
(upon the nets and
in the cabbage
leaking the tweezers'
gaze)

november 2017

sound ritual number 26

chews the apartment, just
for fun, since he was
a senator in a future life.

furniture wife. teakettle stains
on itswallows rug walls reminis
cence at commandhand, vomit

tripleshots of bar bourbon
and longneck bottles of Bud
at Mabuhay Gardens, 1979.

punk rug arrest flats in fuzzy
rooms clawing the walls roaring
trashcan vibration strewn stream

november 2017

sound ritual number 27

suspiciously republican behalf, think
not to be indeed Descartes,

as bad as this was we were
ostensibly conducted in full disclosure.

wobbly wine. grays to the T thclosure. puzzle
we were as bad as this Descartes disappears

into the nearest War-Malt,
without making any noise at all.

november 2017

sound ritual number 28

deciphered memories gathered signals
from rewritten electrical code.

a chip in the brain is worth two in the bush.

birth tooth in a bash.
Bukowski in the bathtub.

hearth bash whisky risky in the icysink
concen trate singularityc hips mass awash koola
id

a hip in the rain is not worth double in the pain

"Wine wine whine"
toilet. blackbirds pecking

ciphered signals code no~ode memories im
plantedc hips turn rom electoral electrocution
birdbath

birdbrain runs the world
sang Allen Ginsberg with The Job
at Le Disque on Haight Street
in 1981

november 2017

sound ritual number 29

atmospheric forecast
precipitates
expressivity thrown
into the New River La
Nina normalcy
blazing fairly crooked
futures rivers of doubt
bleak wor[l]d inhabiting
badly
the snow the shovel
the birds the birdseed
light wind from the east
prophesies arising from
butterflies loosely in ear
nest connect the plots
the kneebone to the
moonbone blots to lots

november 2017

sound ritual number 30

winter occurred
in the growing ladders
below rainfall distributed
signifiers fear of uneven
variability, between the Pacific
Ocean and the Roanoke
Valley Snowy socks Shovel
in a dance before brokenarms
can occur rowing laddersstopped
too late comes too soon wishbone
it is a Friday in mid-November
and i have spent the afternoon
reading poems by Bukowski & Kyger

november 2017

sound ritual number 31

from a glass of water
unless you take the pickled salmon
to the goddess
our poems are based
on the myths of other poems
from the mountain shrill salmon
goddess on a hot rod cloud gas
to speaking lightly of those who ills
actively refusing crimson water
duty pickled asphalt floatsat
'query delite' flight hold it hold going
on like this will get us as always
to where we are 8 P.M. and
the Spurs game is coming on

november 2017

sound ritual number 32

photos puddling
faces in crowds ink
paddling nvestmen
dance it out shredded
words goreing nowhee
exploring the dharma
junket tightrope
traditional tripwire
futures face dancing
puddles blink nowhere
the staged windhowls
thru the picture dripped
d
  r
    i
     pp
        i
         n
           g

november 2017

sound ritual number 33

ashworn brume and bosky
scamplay   stains & trope
wreathe'd about th first farwell
 earthorns, thinhorns, henstorms
intentional and simultaneous
is what they mean by day to day.
we also see the evenings
culminate
in vacuum cleaners and volcanoes.

november 2017

sound ritual number 34

looping de loopop sky,
meaning turning on thground,
brassy arf the hissing trees
circular craning dusting blue
Mole Hill, Ugly Mountain
pyroclastic suitcase
taconic, oceanic
kimberlite moonwater daring basalt reactivation
diamond sword damask   soon wait pyrolite fire
loop by fire
bean by fire
class by fire
role by fre
pyre by fire
burl by fire
berm by fire
mound by fire
poem by volcanic expulsion classroom alarm
the moon dares us to speak about it

november 2017

sound ritual number 35

blue striped ice-face
tones ethereal
feather
drifting magnified
quavering
cloister in each chord
missing did feel disappear
ance in each hand scaling
rope in road the cold can
yon wall
blue jones leather sifting quasar
stippled each the real
magnificent veering
reel
hissing in the goad

november 2017

sound ritual number 36

times honied confusion
years th ingrown rituals
i once got the kind that stop,
the kind that live under the sub
way
    conceptu
al natural ec
stacy
 station

but slivered puzzled aves.
intrude les
papers admitting
sun corseless head,
Icarus,
buried in our memories
are the unit
structures of a war
down under worry

november 2017

sound ritual number 37

peril of minute choice
anew in relative
telepathy
excurse their rhythms
resounding microscopic
conceptu
al natural ec
stacy
but slivered puzzled aves.
intrude les
papers admitting noth
hing hanging on them
relative telepathic peril
rhythm rebounds
rocks on rubber
bounce th towns

no curse eir hythms
not anew as the
crows carry on
the sun cut throat

memories are
mispronounced
soldiers,
kenotaphion,
the empty elsewhere
suitcases
...coffee cups

november 2017

sound ritual number 38

warm snapshot
one hell been
 ago flan
ders pop
pies
flies over the hayfield
and lands on the front porch
of the farmhouse
trap doors
and fried chicken whiskey
pop ders over
easy.
The Mekons
went to Art School
in Leeds.
grabbers mine strike

paper clubbing cold
armbag left over ear
ring toner pouch grin
tat in mourning shiver
.
We Love Our Customers.
Packages Designed
With You In Mind.
granny-grabbers
armchair wing-hat
wine bubbling cleft
tonic mountain.

november 2017

sound ritual number 39

Warm snap shot tonic mountain
was a hell white sheep
flan armchair hat
Pop Boomer grabbers
Pop Ring Toner Task Grin
easy armbag left ear
Mekons Paper arrived
for school education
at Leeds thrust pegs
Quiche With You In Mind
flies over the horses
and the fronts of the Front
Packages Designed the farmhouse
We live our customers Doll with
sadness and fried chicken whiskey

november 2017

sound ritual number 40

Warm Mekons Paper arrived
nap shot mountain hell
was a white sheep
rumchair hat Pop Boo
merflan a grabberson
Pop Rom ba gleft ear
for sching To school
easy rool ed tuner
 Task Grincation
at Leeds trust pegs Doll
Quiche With our Mind
game belies owner Task Griner the
Packages and the fonts   of   the
Designed whisktonic
the farm Fronthouse
We live our customers
shoes sores with
frisadnessed chicken ey?

november 2017

sound ritual number 41

the long supple pihis
the nuemourly du ne
the tandem humming pihis
then scree across the misty
the airfields of archetypal pihis
them lune drossings catapulted hispi
thee horizon gives faith to the pharmacies
them thatdocan bloch droop orangelike goo
maybe before WWI, I don't know
create explosion orb, here's to mist
thought is juxtaposed and sutured
mind is synapses and ruptured
religion has remained simple, like punctuation
pidigion less than themple crock, like dog ma car dies
a gap in our reading
an apt in our treating
automobiles bleating and mourning
morningbleating auto mobiles cele-
ballet jump-cut linear haiku
-rating crump-shut circular goofoffs
transportation is naked and swift
standing onstage na-ked and swift dream
the neck of the poem, in taverns
sun cut asunder in the poems, the light
climbing the clock we saw ourselves astonished
facing the swoon we turn on ambro, descending
the shoes of the sirens glowing on the shore
this rise of the dawning pencil case, in a bag i tore,
november 20, 2017

sound ritual number 42

genre rugged pelvis tugged
recombinatory spirits splint nubis
luggage eggs swiftly poached
olive iris oil stories
horizontal cudgel battle bugle
molten bolts bolts enmolts
melting yolks selling dopes
sun grunts forest clear
soap arpeggio dirt agoneao
coiling bricks roiling trickster
umbrella bacillus trading cluster
cheddar immaculate saint cheese
halogen cask buff rite mask
oblique formica cominique microphone

november 2017

sound ritual number 43

in one says unrelentless demos, the
music of reality,
detuned sense a surprise release
denatured reality coming thruwarp
andwoof as tucked into the songor
sound unbuckled and straitening for
a wall cage into
headbanger ball
room
dancing masks surfictional realty
("there is real real estate out there"
said Terence McKenna)

november 2017

sound ritual number 44

embrac embrouchur emake use of whisper
tagging himundhere manifestation and
souper fluid; as amusers and there a voice
of their exodus fellows and the pieces
one's doubletongue cigeoel'ool !p op
dippers if useless remakes em space
brochure and infestation of humidifiers
lagging invoiced heresy and music boxes
lucid coup; pisces therein flows exiting dust
bunnies plop the frog torque rubble bone.

november 2017

sound ritual number 45

ti on anines how many damp
9 Art 9, , 331 i ific nineteen
ance of the sscusses fragrant
 the sign ere essential ticks
to d Duc p the art of maham cart
kinappropriad kidnapped
 gart in the agduerepro mayhem
ti c on DuchaMa melp r cel Dupont
, Fra Marcel the signifier
, 19 society, the grown trance
Manychamp the nine tie on

november 2017

sound ritual number 46

leaks change and parcel face
shape tub valves minnow snap
raucous what wink pillow

tho fan pire mantic surf
the rise of the serif
serf o man pyre fanatic

pillcep win that faucets
win ow cap values rubs cape
place Marcel in chance beaks

november 2017

sound ritual number 47

your sot ford zero
sleep soda torah
secant est. hut

o lunar mile
o sobar spore
ran chain o sound

lay leg wound rain
cough splant snore rebar
grisnud mi sonar

replace nut crest
tun tibah coda
ekiL 0 forgot

november 2017

sound ritual number 48

double old heat name tone
stuffed my fly lint pelt
at cow erhs reh seal

frog your buyoum nate peak
clay fog score curd folded
nice fin shot red pirate

doorknob mighty rice ponies
surfing moldy play felt
at cheek yr fog unveil

soggy reveal a creak
slay melt suffer colder
dice phone doudoub nightly

november 2017

sound ritual number 49

le th no Achilles
no ríen chartreuse alfalfa
'ni mueren' mirror visage

'mis güevos' socket tuner
no a der nose thunder
rock tuna mist glue voice

'mi visaje nor murmuring
affreuse c'est' not nothing
ekiL 0 Lethe north

november 2017

sound ritual number 50

le th noth th
do not laugh no nothing
'Neither die' 'Ni mueren'

'My güevos' 'Put güevos'
my gloves grievance glue
no to der no toad ear
rock tuna flock puma

'My vision 'Mi visaje
affreuse c'est ' is awful'
ekiL 0 Oh ekiL 0

november 2017

sound ritual number 51

a walrus is not classicism
it is equal to the proletariat
no tilt
Iwo Jima embellished
after The Wasteland
never ending
protest and longing
forest and cutting
huge timber gaps
to fill ones throat
with saw dust
with Kremlin chapstick
between the silent milks

november 2017

sound ritual number 52

1.

becoming one with the undone hallu
cination, a reflection
of the diagonal order
is already mostly on the table
sofast under the hands carded &dealt
winning slip shots stringy rug machines
formulaic thru the waters of sound clipper
grabber mirrors and the undone mask ro
-tating

2.

silver paperthin cold arm
lip   wit shivers the book
ing band pulse sesdynamic
flight   quails in sight
's turningup imploding   axis
my ax istrumpet
becoming one with the undone hallu
cination, a reflection
of the diagonal order
is already mostly on the table

sound ritual #53

throughout the ancient
dangers
Lock up yoThe richta X
the near measure slants
small caroms rotate
open hands
attached by language
by kora, balafon, n'goni
to seashells
daughterseeC   brea k. ?The rich
scripted ancestors
they jelly pirate patrons from
g a   P
GO   P   ',
morPhonster
a frenzy of motels
and exiles
otherthan this
estimated linguistic
sideways
a mist comes
speaking plucked formations
& single string fiddles
deemboomIto
Wassoulou
Chicago
and you

november 2017

sound ritual number 54

highway anodyne parachutes
light on peptic side arm
words diffe above it
thflare feet popsickle push
        flame
          legume
      daisey coot
Perspex themselves
whose cavities abscond
pestulant daisy pusspout
pods fauna civilizatic legs

november 2017

sound ritual number 55

masks of sound
    and tarotic unrest
under a curvilinear seaside
scoups of flies
     all buzzcouping frenzy
toward a herculuckier portside
Popeye snoops
        sclerotic
          unbound
Hercules inscapes fuzz
so what then
              neurotic
                unwound
Paraclete fuzz shaped jazz
     Paracelsus
         Bird
      alchemy
praise-songs of the heretics
burning at their stakes

november 2017

sound ritual number 56

metallicitrus
fairtopluckout
realism, indeed, drowns
in the causal literature
portentious claghazes
metallicitrus jet lag capital
statistical fructifying
pedagogy underscoring
impeccable
underscores
  floopa loo ping
  coot machines
preposterous
enjoyment
ridiculous
employment

november 2017

sound ritual number 57

tangibly seamed
maw oft songs
between never kelp
clamor accord
rupture equation
crass squawk linear
duck crossing atth line
plenum color tonight jo
key troubadour's harbor
abducent abraxis gongs
graten ear ive rosben dong
gone too long never kelp comes home.
legible claw between clamp rapture
class pluck plectrum ley lines
adjacent grated parmesan
lone dreams soft longing
fever clip equators
quack lineated
croissant
tonight

november 2017

sound ritual number 58

"in fish are the reasons of fish.
why do you need to know?"
these lines by themselves in
an email file, had something
to do with what? the rhumba
last year at th aquarium club
fish dance frenzy did i see?mid
'round nightfish unhooked
some but not all escaped
leaps of inventoried field trips
kinetic muse irrigated boardroom
salt design, chairs aligned holistic.

november 2017

sound ritual number 59

1.
guz zler lung tu lip arrest defacto linens
sweater short nudges collision quarks posted
''never the flash again sd._ bibliomancy gus
the underburner pinch'd, the toad eye sound
remembered, the saltimbanques utopia prkway'd.
cited unmapped avant-obscurity / acclaimed
seaside penguin fiction / verdict next body pier
breakdown / edenic horse property registered
obsession / in addition chosen photographic /
venues teenager metafictional prose "hello"

2.
self as runaway explication often of
guz zler lung tu lip arrest defacto linens
drift diffe mezzotints awkwardness
sweater short nudges collision quarks posted
personal visigoth and sacrificial restraint
''never the flash again sd._ bibliomancy gus
the absurd narrowness of organic exhaust"
the underburner pinch'd, the toad eye sound
imaginary boundaries loosely inevitable
remembered, the saltimbanques utopia prkway'd.

november 2017

sound ritual number 60

plate the tall fish like a mix of minutes
with juniper berries liquefy
the fire.
eyeballs cog on a farm, earthquake
just hap
serie
on a stool
the safest p.
collap were zone thought simultar
uranus map on the counter eye
pullies
harse serie har pull
speries feetdown to clog in a firm
shaking junitarfish stake handle
then thin spool aquake a mi nute flic
quakes the dollfish a pixie mutes
snakefilm Jupiter
clots hearse Harpies lull

november 2017

sound ritual number 61

while and chose, it
conceives a dystopian contemporary,
plentiful furniture for everyone.
simulacrum, even
in the shoe, the shoe, the shoe,
west of exterior, had been given.
sutra   close & while inthere chew
thesimu la crumshoe, stuckgum
wad in dust   shoe ,dis toppee
fountain fontanel montane
dog shoe sutra and blind side picks
glum topping inherent crew
lighter on the in when and pick, interrior
dyspepsic furniture sit uati ons   later
think up plan et one all seated,
in a fein faint shoe eruption, it
surrounds the sun with lake codex
houses unearthed tomorrow and
dissolved to travel our blurring
sensibilities,

november 2017

sound ritual number 62

sun, ticks details   to the   groundust
plenum standards flee, starshit the distance
clover closures marilyn passes sun's fever
dance wicker balsam funeral rites shamaniac
platter, caribou drilling in the dangerous
congress. coal voices hosting gerrymandered
aluminum, banana peels and boat-trip
pathogens. archaeological misdemeanors
amid the scrap verges ajar playful none
shanks from odd nerdstrum a hialclas
sicattack, bargesthat run ashore, apple sauce
that warms, concrete that splinters, amnesiac
generation , found some air, tick s tick s tick.

november 2017

sound ritual number 63

how can we circulate the teeth-knolls
obtuse research exhumed
at the border of merz and sapphire?
how can Expositor debunk   the hub garnishments
flowers the wilt of gravy wriggly research'd eyes
omens' sons corn   house salamander under shoes?
narrow passages loosely sliver the thumb cheese
bordering bau & coal. dust
roots proxy compounding
predators
roofing nails by the bucket
Baul poets on a Dylan cover
"history has a stutter / it says w w w w watch out!"

november 2017

sound ritual #64

teeth my lipnet, garage lipcaulk spinner
shining nail in my heel, the dabbloc brings
flooded forets no nests to run inno needfor fall
teether comes1st teaser troutbilly, my LiPo
LiFo, calibrated neck the liquefiedom
collects. rigin of Bab test. therust
tooth shipping bloodied breething life boat
collates derelict myth failing comets combs
celebrated rigidity of leap year in gnostic
love fests greasing the wreck fabulous
slipwalkers diabolic innocence and ruin,
trouble in the liquid kingdom (in petrodollars
they no longer trust) rust (crustacean
spanner sings feed for the ball)

november 2017

sound ritual #65

voice of arrangers arranged
elusive lamp marimba
diagonal witchdoctor rhythm
roots are routes, gutbucket
piss & oil, evading light cong
as we doubletongue and fluttr
tongue arrangers of pierced voices,
snake charters hiss and coil,
pervade the night and congre
gate, rubble sponge and mutter
upon derangement, piers and
jettys invoiced kublah kahn &
john cage, you had yr chance
the mouthpiece is a 7C & the
bore of the   bone is medium large
(coriander, C-clamp, colander)

november 2017

sound ritual 66

cara mel strum for cover by
lem on high grass to reckon
frenzied frac tured space clot
standard stoppages wince coy

there are hilum enzymes
standing in our meal
thigh vacuum stop watches
fork and beckon
spice wine plots the toy

burrbl grit the splat of decibals
tubular eye clouds lost cawmeal
walls that serve at curves shrink
forest chugging catalogues, pills

november 2017

sound ritual 67

original taste in vocalizing points to
auteurs and aircraft, close listening
to the ridges of several feathers
beside a stepladder so much dep ends

janky stand pelters   grip the crogh cre
eping lurch spindles   trmpetsunday   flo
p ping   voice containers top ping stream robo
nips cheeselink eye pullies goofly   open'd off
teary blank photographs   plonk in the sluice
pages, one too many salty swift and not goodbye,
feather tips, code talkers' taste in closinzg songs

november 2017

sound ritual 68

the meat philosopher for grinder's impossible
layers immediate everyday clothes a puzzle
with no solution is a mystery the ''m eat grin
der's iron clothing'' iron curtains creep
ing axels pinge moss nerves across
the border skin sleep punk dreamer
casts peculiar pink stay in swift paper a rena
castyr nets, castaways, castinets paper cloud
potter
plotters duce cards gone the ceiling blew for
tune's cookies
1) sulfur
2) immolate
----------------------soluble
----------------------fish
                    [iron shirt...
                    ...mass, curves]
                 l
                  ea
                    p
                    in
                      g
   caper   loud   blotter's   dice

november 2017

sound ritual # 69

bornagain clamsalv ation's   lob
feelstheoncoming 0 tocotta o felt
lobstererss, only the frail fogharbor
sag eros leaves supple baker's cut
slanted chameleon's news paupers
...wind rose sours the later round,
cup and glut swarming nocturne,
b'asswind be Ll e -fssss fusssy
snaky blue heron techper fish
fect spirit notune(warm snugun
sup & around,/ the water pours,
whose wine? newsalv
(camelemon scented,
    ((but fake apples eve zonezero

november 2017

sound ritual number 70

mindsliding blue constant
loopylake back of beyond
acoustic mutation lingering
clogged becoming glance
nonlinear anthropocene
fractura solinas as gander
evolve perpetual models
fruit ear sticky veilshat floats
consumption g# suite   win
dow provocatively nestled
rubicon mist planetx downstream
flamboyant data goopsake
streamingred mouth b&wdetails
mesmerizing floating noise
percolation falls frommich so
exceeds prevalent peels
lookfor outsposted detritusslivers
permutations spellbound now to
block tansion riots in synapses,
blink bolinas sail-vat cons
gumption silicon derails
from mage deconstructs silver
tension in griot syntax

november 2017

sound ritual 71

traceneth   sayto hip changes
a letter a wordgnippers pantsdept.
smite gnoshes ashes salad foo t
growth around grope th
ese days, frays knees around
rope grout soot sailing hashish
from the Hôtel de Lauzun
To 9 Rue Gît-le-Cœur. might the
deep slant of wordslippage change
the letteral to a trance of the unsaid?
then, squeezeth   greebewathplug
kment dexterity eyeboaring pausedustbon
gring instruct , wallowthis- in the pasty blur
rotasting rant, ''damp clamp" "dampc lamp"
"damcl amp" roasting plant tasty blurt
swallow the hiss Faust cause born
eye-boarding water-boring flexterity
green bean warthog squeeze quiz breath

november 2017

sound ritual number 72

an immediate fauna of citizens
from the natic capita grounding
salt and devolo made knovvn
at the intersection of lungs and
cheese, drafty shorts, plyaways
away, always, plywood, woodbine,
Parthenocissus quinquefolia,
Virginia creeper, Parthenocissus
tricuspidata, Japanese creeper,
Parthenocissus vitacea, thicket
creeper, false Virginia creeper,
brine, salt, milk, Hittites, salary,
salad, emperor, formula, melting,
cheese riveatstunt ed streaming
creeper (((river, reaper, riveted:
creed, geese, stunt man united)

november 2017

sound ritual number 73

whisky pierce feckless air crinkled misty rub
lacking initiative or strength of character; irresponsible
virtue gear Oslo fid a been net scratched fasmoving
To the north and east, wide forested hills (Marka) rise
frugal fugal fungal flugle flu e gel rextram inter
of, relating to, or having the characteristics of fungi
ludes eatrasizing perf. Pr. P dext. pluckedwhisky
a downer, a depressant, similar to barbiturates
pierce feckless air crinkled misty rub
late 16th century: from Scots and northern English
dialect feck (from effeck, variant of effect) + -less.
virtue gear Oslo fid a been net scratched fasmoving
In 1174, Hovedøya Abbey was built. The churches and
abbeys became major owners of large tracts of land,
frugal fugal fungal flugle flu e gel rextram inter
mid 16th century: from Latin frugalis, from frugi
'economical, thrifty,' from frux, frug- 'fruit.'
ludes featuring emphasizing perf. Pr. P dext. plucked
late Old English ploccian, pluccian, of Germanic origin;
related to Flemish plokken ; probably from the base of
Old French (es)peluchier 'to pluck.' cment dexterity
eye boars th dust ring instructions Middle English:
from Old French ciment (noun), cimenter (verb), from
Latin caementum 'quarry stone,' from caedere 'hew.'
installations adjusted pivot shorts dunk'd end kicks
from French, probably from the root of dialect pue
'tooth of a comb' and Spanish pu(y)a 'point.'
cment dexterity eye boars th dust ring instructions
a tusked Eurasian wild pig from which domestic pigs
are descended. the full-grown male of certain other
animals, especially a badger, guinea pig, or hedgehog.
installations adjusted pivot shorts dunk'd end kicks, o

november 2017

sound ritual number 74

million on July chief refined December
new foremost line and cures
songs still collagen under the early
finds / late falls amillion curesrarified
foremost leaven eggbeater thresholds
redefine December nostrils & eyes
premeditated gusto repeats paternal
retrovirus / ultimate parataxis seconds
mandarin Buick quill and olives /
quite feverish scree parasol studious
frenchmen observe on the rue home /
chief on collagen drills and December
million lopping courses they flew, one
for another / it was cold with no line
of battle / banana drums / Julius Caesar
umbrellas, cornetrains, JCsalads beat
and / traffic cones, John Coltrane, brillo

november 2017

sound ritual number 75

proto forma robo reamer facies
rays catchers rice day bobblers
cornets sounders van debt de
posers thin sidewalk creasers
poked umbrella upshot discourses
patronage Cambodia fed by air
as much Bangkok unmarked arms
assets delivered opium control
warriors border plotting ensconced
mainland troops & mountain camps
information tube   kleksovaniye
in herentTvorsky chunk bio- impulses
former human personality structuring
mezhprotoformnaYa wild facilitatesolaroat
mainland, cheesemelt 7th sense red sound
a vacant color
Nixon
profit monopoly from malaria poppy
        spread   smoking   traders   native
heroin the supreme opponent
    fieldsmilitaryplanmoney
crop   taxpayers'   advantage
f r a c t i o n of d e s t r o y e d situations
bugger phonelast din ner smoking denpop
dinnerfix last flax laugh, walking co m m,a detailspirt,
lungfooT, daisy quill, lilly toe, fig., A 5, "foamy licewoo,d cage,
[john]mtn lake campscrowding fire, forma terra's peel & burn
   Tvor sky, 'hooded Bonegrit

december 2017

sound ritual number 76

the fortunes reached
6,500 tons

foamy rosehips special/
ascension by dinner fix

last flax laugh,walking detailsXpirt,
lungfoot, daisy quill, lilly toe,

fig.A 5"foamy policewood cage/,
British hiked 1858 China essential respects compensation for

British government the treaty
fun damental updatingmindcounts

military after population, including
China 27 percent 1840 there Chinese

slaughtering hundreds open to bloody
cosmic mary human flavored koolaide

Campaigns.

december 2017

sound ritual 77

smouldering place, gulf
my mind, rusty cough off/
spat against the coin, dew
y chestnut shunt, the strait

--where we find ourselves,
in front of a specific poem,
ou / ou / ai oi / ai, is where
we start looking, thinking in
vowels and consonants...
ul ul / us ug / / ut unt... no
ideas but in, but in what?--

strait the shunt,   unt, ult, ust
chestnuttyraw dew coin coughoff,
in what? in what? where ie mys
terious ul, ou, oioi auiaui idea,
fuckgreetrs of the dead finger

--but there is no ult. only uld ulf /
ust ugh / / ut and unt. exult! the
result is no fault of the poem.

december 2017

sound ritual number 78

aum-vehicle
horn sounding
loudly no parking
data in February 105 years
when we last five seasons
s warming OMb strict rations
for the poor probability distributions
storm of probabilities, endless candy ghosts
given out as treats along the volcano rim rom
low snow decade of decline
meteorological looming
toads grooming in swampmap flavor, an
insouciant bass, birdsong grasses
song hari krishna,
yeshua. trumpet clause
double slit experiment, delayed choice
quantum eraser experiment, PEAR labs, Emoto
rice experiment, placebo-nocebo, Waking Life,
Manifesting the Mind, MAPS, Living Matrix,
TED: meditation, lucid dreaming, fasting,
bands; beats, yoga nidra, tummo,
tulpa, lung gom pa, natural law,
science of lucid dreaming,
binaural bodhisattva,
beats Don Quixote
'tilting at windmills

december 2017

sound ritual number 79

1.
micro-examples mainly
tax advantage, even dividuals
will be phased out
murder by de(c)gree d
ta ned communiti
altum statum continuiii

2.
negative $1.5 trillion what
about the working class
we are many they are few
take over
Washingtor we'r v politio
      savy

3.
future beyond government
rigging grassroots
disease giveaway
cronies donors plutocracy
horriblc powerfu mone
arch rulers sons beasts
religious
brain synapses

december 2017

sound ritual number 80

3am muddied graymoon ihear

that sound ritual, the jazz
    dark night
keys voice

  Ascending
        better get hit in your soul
 gentle hand

    lowering slightly
          ah um
sung into the moon,

december 2017

sound ritual number 81

the front door burns
the sireens in my head,''
the basement rises,
the familiar window irises
hushed

each morning, nothing
much

a new crisis from anywhere

cuts across the couch
and dusts the desk

screen,
mulch, chrysalis,
Everywhere

december 2017

Sound Ritual 82

be there at 6
local events
gig at 8 sharp
wanted that
gee)unload loadin
excessive
sound checkat 6
for doing
6 sharp   #
believed
allwear holey jeans
every minute
t-shirts uniformlook
festivals
\\''we are going as
notes & comments
'garth brooks
apostrophe
does
zappa &
james brown

december 2017

sound ritual number 83

playfulness that are
come gold milk practice
prose, wringer
poet, st.vitus,
the official album
box and one potentially
1 unit of free will
insisting, than

the eleven officially,
more removed the ssever
dhead from the suitcase

emergence of predicament
smoke slips fingers mind mint
reading about toes, tides
fish tracks and other secrets,
an independent sea

adhere to any sequence
these words syntax out
unable, playfulness that are
improvisations recognizably enable
communion, commitment
engaging, also, the fire
raging heart
literary plus pianists
call the shits   a
coconut abandon

sunlight. nutrients. combat. disrepair.
eats strategic dance
moonlight in abeyance now
decades understood sense
keening favored ''heartshapes
valley rather fidgets now among pilgrims,
the human burlap hearts

december 2017

sound ritual number 84

In the faucet pulsing gauze, mir
o/red
be lie fs be gon
   Barrier Canyon pictographs
         5600 b.c.e.
      forms pomegranate Reagan

digestive thundering trees inflated
   large eyes, horns, or antennae
         The Maze variant is characterized
by an extreme stylization and elongation of the figures,
      in Eyes unlike coal

muddy rinse dance digested   hole
   bird, snake, and plant spirits
         Figu and p resen Figu
      unprocessed unique dawns
       bell leafs began

lens eye pullies ear thorns vertiginous artauddouble
commode spent spine
   muted greens, yellows, blues and black
         hybrid style line within large holy ghost
      ed phic betw brush Occam spray soul Razor
       shoe leather eidetic Bush regime

lease winds ride hothit numb mind boots load loot
"finished knowing then"
   Although the forms of the spirit
         figures are similar the paint application
      techniques suggest that many were painted

in Contra
different time-periods
      (circa 6,750 b.c.e.
   to circa c.e. 300)
.

december 2017

sound ritual number 85

tinker creek to analyze emotional
grid connections paralysis under
  inspection in the elemental
      selection agencies overseeing

commercial surveillance under
feedback delimiting protected service
  violations in cheesy
      selective site- bones backtracking

hegemonic reselling bent mountain
exhausted non-rigid sunsets pow
  corrective actions   er the network
       select screams finding the future

yttrium, hafnium, movable bridges,
covered bridges, ridding, swamped
   Y-Hf ound hidden secretions gre
        spec sle lun boc jaah jaah

to
             the drubn rant,
                                              o
how
     much longer will i be able
             to
inhabit   the
          divine sepulcher

december 2017

sound ritual number 86

dual narratives bit extu al sans kri
Copenhagen baggage
t syntax army life of bendex riley tv
  xXx
      //\\\/\\////\\\\
          ||||
before two bands in Boston. crash the commons
net neutrality rising, by train,
t wo different marches, 2 diff keys teevee life ed sull
  xXx
      //\\\/\\////\\\\
          ||||
ives sat on the loose grass. pigeons encampment.
in 22 minutes, what a marvel
memoryunto a twoer lava lamp. pitcairn& the canary dave garr

december 2017

sound ritual number 87

garage was still purple flabby goodbye
dead fish growing the baby's dirt road
famished jeans har bored and port stitches
skiboardsbathing garage sessions ban
dingspoon-crossed corbeil, blue phlox,
tufts of sofa-milk light

livid chestnuts shuddering a thimble
cross hairs in a balloon har harse th
phantom lamuettes phish ade silly silo
let not add, impediments slinky hollow

Persephone, the warrior, the the
underworld toilet there sto
pped ish drain collusio in te elo dump

parallel membranes string-on, soldier,
lossaround louse saround this   head
this house (made of card((s)) bored?)
the kelp-lamp and forceps
absolute strip mall algebra
in hell
on its heels
help!

december 2017

sound ritual number 88

disturbia clack to eden's tree
zoo shoes energy
syllable spit

spitsnaker barbequed error
fuzzy apocalypse energy
syllable pipe

pipeline fish alarmscaly gutty
rowdy suburbs energy
syllable fish

a high-energy construct and an energy-discharge
flounder, on toast lawnsprinkled
streaked sun energy
rest stop energy
yarrowhertz energy
ostranenie energy
the wrinkled dawn energy
syllable bop

bap tazer ostrungdisturbia now
Laramie, Scranton energy
(will have some several causations)
syllable freak

freakystun restgo yemahahtz
snake skit energy
Disputanta energy
grayscale energy
syllable back

back to growly burbbled skies
coiled zodiac lips energy
syllable gray

graysodas puz zlescol lapse
rosin roast ripe ruts energy
syllable zoo

,Zooz of gods
barbarian queue energy
syllable disturbs

december 2017

sound ritual number 89

neutrality such as stones in the previous never slab,
assurance the fork ale slashed neutered marker, rather
to slapfish in Colorado on the door
oppose to slur daisies pastiche coral

ineffable opposition whereas priority cliffhanger/
stunstones ofsuch as Colorado pullscapable, then
asylum red port system-to-eye
not seeing clear -lye- mail- sand
resounding stilts yucca
powder flows undo on toast
opposition whereas forktines
scrunch the tinfoil flounder

flattened sandwich across
pullslye toaster's tonguetines
the road buds android ants
insurance slurps the sunflowers
bent pestilence serenade to

expox the top betting mirrors
trashtakers liquid clear finders
ash from the Pepsi portfolio,
the peptic shoe, the oval lips
bloc x-ray constituency depicts wax-flash data

december 2017

Sound Ritual 90

bugger line the uninhabitable shoe,
mugger, burglar, cat-muggler, wine,
the old lady who lived with
a thousand obnoxious kids, in a
shoe, habitual bitumen unable

doling out sit uation peacocks in daisies
live Actionist role-players in Vienna,
citations in situ, Vishnu split-peas
in socks, the days are as they say
they are, sleep-gradations on the clock

snow downed, slurfluss speech at the begin,
on the begin, in the begin, at dawn
the plows blur custard and peach,
peach brother, from the bully culprit

rote frown triage horses noted diameter ring
mileage gown mote string theoretical
diamonds bloated curse and hearse
rot smote down the tragedies horseless boat

december 2017

sound ritual number 91

facts are desires parboiled with dashes
clues then bixblues recent from carp oil
orchestrated mordant photojournalism
dies and stains frequent rests alle grother
realism dreaming amphibian ball-bearings
fish streaming swan cars for rent or sailing
what do poems feel like in a sentence?
prison sentences else a way eelsin foam
the rugride balls misguide pick the numbers
paragraphs, else card-carrying gnomes
cochlear hissing conducted anonymously
immunity breathtakingly hypermodern
orchestrated edges leaps yellow chakra tern
at quarry thin parking lots combinatory sleeps

december 2017

sound ritual number 92

buzzard wings uber tiny roof banquet bouquet
amniotic liminal botany
Mojave agitprop spillage

gives way raniers dust dance or upspan began
continuous project altered daily
sortilege subrealized making markings

on cool hiway exists in memory no good any mote
huddled wobbly glimpses, ecstatic phrases
initiate intimate
indeterminate
in the dance limited my physical pleasure of move, went
atmospheric hymns migrate catastrophe
obscure reminder flocking rainbows
wave-snap muscle punctuates

concept of dust
no longer from where also quite
people working context to meanings
let's talk suspension already immediacy

''how do you look
recites the news
concept of amniotic buzzard cartilage
mitigates kaleidoscopic glimpses

when there' nothing left to move''
wings liminal dust raining daily

december 2017

sound ritual number 93

safety isolation sky adapting worrying rhythms
everything teaches obsess circulates golden
handcuffs velvet rut roots in the basic fabricant

basics intuitive factory animate learning angles
hidden settled accumulation invaded dozen quit
quizzes lofty positions that claim discourse won

talking classes social lexical happy sparked
entertained transformative other challenges
gluey tendons applied with nail polish although

boast order ghost importance who disappointment
was emerging letters referendum causal stability
unsaleable gestures toward animate factory worry

liberals emergency eternity destiny lemur striking
mortal varied themselves events liberated theatrical
rhetorical ba ka sheut ib liberates shot shoot sun cut

vulnerable combing throughout serial traveled
wonder soon proprioceptive redress mind gathers
reception   yellow flame   the wax runs low

contradictory identifying felt describes become
worry movements taki tiva dance uncut uncuffed

december 2017

sound ritual number 94

serial emergency eternity destiny lemur throughout
combing varied themselves events liberated vulnerable
cut ba ka sheut ib liberates shot shoot sun rhetorical
dance teaches obsess circulates taki tiva
runs classes social lexical happy the wax
flame transformative other yellow
reception tendons applied with nail polish gathers
wonder gestures toward animate factory traveled
mind order ghost importance who redress
movements velvet rut roots in the basic worry
become intuitive factory animate learning describes
uncuffed isolation sky adapting worrying uncut
felt settled accumulation invaded dozen identifying
contradictory lofty positions that claim discourse low
proprioceptive emerging letters referendum causal soon

december 2017

sound ritual number 95

care mor kind ividuals
are more
knit
di vi du al s

forged fore. . . thse fines
or led
before
as fires

the ll be the day ta
poems
on the page can be
quiet

comma,   pee c
coming
a   part

error move on, b/c
perception
instanter
perception

sd. of them we s linger long er
, slowly
along, slant breath

pinion of doctor he help s end
each ending
a new

syn the syze canmu sicmov arc must
signdust
does not sizzle
and can not mute

rash trackers   rants   ash gaw kers
trash slackers   slants

december 2017

sound ritual number 96

measuring and enumerating blunt shadows
came from
humming tunes
this world
rejected
picks, pikes, spaded lopped mongrel tree trunks
age
in a standing
feather
forms or feels
culminated in an inhabited ring the spiders noserings
rooted. was.
stint spent some mutant hat,
the instance,
about, was
building,
we imagine we see the action captivate thought, neither
after
the direction
of the
most
respected w
a
v
e
s
poet hurtles into matter astral libido formations aware stuck

december 2017

sound ritual number 97

prayer wheel, the 3 cat night
        haecceity dog
    banana nut bread
in sight as rain projects dark surges

   curios frown
          land,
      plume
black drops upon a leaden ground

   weave clay
          pigeons
      foisted
songs grey may be drops dreaming flooding

     lather
         the sun
      with molasses and opal
later catch the sun compass mirrors every oval one

   long may your grey matter hop
      floating beribboned copse
wreathe the squabbling grass pigeons every foible ,any 2 of 2
         inside a brain our wreckage sparks and urges

known curious imperfections tails heads plaintive
      wheel-layer spinning in flames
certainty   un ravel un grounded un leaded dream:
  sanity
is a measure
         of proximity to consensus.

december 2017

sound ritual number 98

observe rice pounding sleep
spitting
pinned
spine
consider elderly ice ticking
normal
formats
formless
slow numb dimensions odorous sky
crumbs
numbering
nimble
imperfect formal scoops: sen iors,
welders
eldritch
elderberries
observe inexplicable rituals spinning
dice
rounders
slip

december 2017

sound ritual number 99

before them darkness no sound
left fingers and come squiggles talk
candles to them

cleft knee
six candles and a crucifix attuned atoned
on to further Freedom rather at,

and a darkness
freak doom
rather a squabble, all that talk at once law elements

earth bone with elements at once
crucifix no
leather & feathers

Freedom elements harmony disintegrates dust squiggles
fragments free a harmony squabble law
attuned sound

wax handles
free tails heads and further with a plaintive certainty, come
scraps tails plaintive disintegrates all elements

atoned
therefore themed
left on earth fragments, scraps trace fingers to bone

trace heads certainty dust that six
before
dark nests

december 2017

sound ritual number 100

work nights the marrow steam the coastal stewing snow
today heights and have drones
not to speak without a blink
borders proven numbers
from Somalia to Pakistan
finger shaking shading shad shiv shit
linger
waking
fading
shade
shivering shirts
white sheets blankets writing freckled clod ashes, before
decided
who multiplied
in the Greater Middle East
swaths made have taken their more
tasting ritual stew exteriorized search stanchion milkdust
wasting
spiritual
few interiorized
perch
standards
silk road
large purse n the 6th soaking the bundle racing murkiness
indisputable fewer sprung failed
instability spread
eliminated ultimately various
disorder encounters
penchant and capacity
purple hearse race far beneath snow   mudlucious fickle up
turtle
horse
rice
fear / breath / cow
mud
luckiest
trickle up

december 2017

A few of the many gnashmiort publications from mOnocle-Lash Anti-Press:

***Soul-roulette: Transmutations of Nerval**, by Gérard de Nerval & Retorico Unentesi.* Experimental and 'pataphysical transductions of poetry by the early avant-gardist Gérard de Nerval, rendered by the mysterious Retorico Unentesi of the Institute for Study & Application, Kohoutenberg. Padded out with extensive front-matter by eminent dead persons and an epic appendix elaborating & tangentiating upon the seams & merging of translation & poetic creation.

66 pgs perfect-bound,Sept., A.Da. 101 (2017). $7.00 + s/h

Wordsworth's "The Prelude; or, I Get Smarter: A Poem About Me"
—Translated into Even-More-Boring-and-Trite by Fast Sedan Nellson

We're proud to release the ***fourth volume*** of the British Post-NeoAbsurdist Fast Sedan Nellson's gleefully spiteful, blatantly unfair, copiously annotated translation of Wordsworth's 230-page autobiographical poem into an obscure dialect of English, 'Even-More-Boring-and-Trite'. The newest installment of a set of 14 volumes, followed by a deluxe perfect-bound edition with parallel translation and extensive introduction and commentary. ***Vol. I:*** "It starts–Being a Kid–Going to School" / ***Vol. II:*** "About School (Even more of It)" / ***Vol. III:*** "I Live in Cambridge" / ***Vol.IV:*** "Summer Break" **NEW**

$1–$2 + s/h per volume–see website. Vol. 4 $2.50 postpaid.

In-Appropriated Press #1–9

A raucous mélange of avant-garde & Post-NeoAbsurdist verbiage, thinkage, collage, reportage, & more from Roanoke, VA & around the globe, with work by Bennett, Leftwich, Lindsann, Musicmaster, Katastrof, Fry, Repass, Dec, Oliver, Birch, Abel, Damerow, Blafas, & many more!

$0.50–$2.50 + s/h per issue–see website. Issue 9 $3.50 postpaid.

& more than 100 other disorienting works – Order at www.monoclelash.wordpress.com

Forthcoming Publications

Images & Words [Title to be Decided]*, by Crank Sturgeon:* A compendium of scrib[l]ings by the hard-touring American noise-maker, performer, and reality-twister Crank Sturgeon.

Poems [Title to be Decided]*, by Edwin Birch*: A long-overdue compendium of linguistic trespasses by the Post-NeoAbsurdest of British versificators.

Exquisite Crypt #4: Chatroom Invasions. Transcript of a 2006 Post-NeoAbsurdist international poetic invasion of an unsuspecting chatroom.

The Horse-Killer: Vol. 2, *by Monk O'Lindsann*. Next installment of the Gothic (Anti-)Novel set in a time/space-dislocated Avant-Garde utopia.

Forthcoming from Revenant Editions

Translations, Republications, & Commentaries on the 19th Century Avant-Garde

Ubu's Almanac, *by Alfred Jarry, translated by Amy Oliver:* (Dis-]orient yourself toward the coming 'pataphysico-symbolico-hermetico-bohemian year with a new translation of Jarry's 1899 annual.

Cinders from 'Fire & Flame', *by Philothée O'Neddy*. New translations from the signature 1833 collection of the Bouzingo co-founder, one of the most influential, yet forgotten, writers of the Romanticist avant-garde. An appetizer for a coming full-length anthology.

The Frenetic Feminine. Texts and images by over a dozen female co-founders of the avant-garde, 1820–1840, many appearing in English for the first time. Including Sand, Mercoeur, Debordes-Valmore, Argoult, Tastu, Waldor, Gay, Girardin, and others.

Incoherent Footprints of the Rabid Black Cat. Anthology of avant-comedy from the overlapping bohemian Incoherents, Hydropathes, and Chat Noir groups, including Allais, Sapek, Verlaine, Lévy, Bilhaud, Godeau, Cros, Salis, Rollinat, Richepin, and others.

www.ingramcontent.com/pod-product-compliance
Lightning Source LLC
Chambersburg PA
CBHW071316040426
42444CB00009B/2026
* 9 7 8 1 9 4 8 6 3 7 0 0 8 *